FRUIT OF THE SPIRIT
31 DAY
DEVOTIONAL

I0159844

Solitude Series
Love

D Yvonne Shotwell

DEDICATION

This book is dedicated to the body of Christ
whom each day the sweet aroma of her godly
fruit is consuming the air we breathe.

ACKNOWLEDGMENTS

I acknowledge the Father, Son and the Holy Spirit as the author of this devotional. I thank God for creating me; I thank Jesus for giving me gifts, and I thank the Holy Spirit for being my life teacher and mentor. This book is written all because of "The Trinity."

DAY 1

Genesis 22.2

Then God said, "Take your son, your only son, Isaac, whom you love, and go to the region of Moriah. Sacrifice him there as a burnt offering on one of the mountains I will tell you about."

There will be times in our lives when God will demand that we give up the thing that we love the most. What could be more precious than a child that came from your seed or your womb? As we look back into the times of Abraham's life we know that having a male child meant everything. But yet God even asked that to be sacrificed to him. It is interesting because Moriah means "Jehovah Provides." Offering sacrifices to God was not something uncommon to the Hebrew people because that is how they kept their right relationship with God. Hebrew sacrificial offering was done by offering animals, grain, etc. According to the Bible, God never told them to offer a human being until he spoke to Abraham. That was what pagans were doing for their gods, especially offering their first born son Even in India and Africa today I have heard that widows are often burned at their husband's burial because of traditional, pagan beliefs. Abraham lived in a pagan and evil society just as we do today. Perhaps Abraham knew that once he was at Moriah it would definitely mean that God had provided an offering through his son Isaac. Although Abraham might not have understood everything, he decided to trust God; though probably not without a struggle. Abraham obeyed God in not only his actions, but also in his heart; Cain (Adam's son) in the earlier part of the book of Genesis gave the outward appearance that he was obedient, but his heart showed us that he was fully disobedient. Man truly looks at the outward, but God looks at the heart. Could it have been that God was testing Abraham to see what he was made of? When God tells us to sacrifice something very dear to us it allows us to know the areas of our strengths and weaknesses and where we have built up idols that have taken the place of God. Personally, the most difficult sacrifices God required of me was to give up my desire for marriage and to accept the call of God on my life. They weren't easy decisions, but after several months of battling with God's requests, I relented and decided that obeying God was better than even marriage and following my own life plans. As it relates to marriage, immediately after I gave in, the Lord said I just wanted to see if you were willing. So today, I ask, "Are you willing to lay ALL on the altar of sacrifice for the Lord"? God asks you to surrender all because of his love for you, but your obedience shows your love to him. Seek him in prayer now. Maybe he wanted to teach Abraham to know his voice more clearly. Perhaps, he wanted to see if Abraham loved him more than the most valued possession in his life, his one and only son. I find this quite significant because God asked Abraham to do what he himself was actually going to fully carry out by offering his one and only son, Jesus Christ, as a sacrifice for our sins on the altar of the cross so that we would have a right relationship with Him.

Prayer: Father God, thank you for offering your only son Jesus Christ as a sacrifice for me on the cross so that my sins are now washed away and I am clean and can come to you without guilt, but with all grace, in Jesus name, amen.

DAY 2

Exodus 20.5-6

You shall not bow down to them or worship them; for I, the LORD your God, am a jealous God, punishing the children for the sin of the fathers to the third and fourth generation of those who hate me, but showing love to a thousand [generations] of those who love me and keep my commandments.

I wanted to only give verse 6, but as I thought upon this I realized that it becomes more powerful when kept in context with verse 5. I think we can really appreciate God's love when we realize how sinful we are and how long God has put up with our sins. The King James Version says "visiting the iniquities of the fathers upon the children." Iniquity is sin, but it is often the most evil and wickedness of sin. It is the sin of the generations of our family even to the third and fourth generations. And that is not a good inheritance in case you have any doubt. God hates sin as we can see and the consequences of sin have to be paid for. Have you ever wondered when you look into some families and you see a generation of preachers and strong Christians? That is the generational blessing. And I am sure that you have seen others who seem to have a continuous cycle of what seemingly appears to be a curse. Sometimes people will even remind themselves that they are cursed by saying things such as, "You know manic depression runs in my family or we always have been poor for as long as I can remember, even my grandmother says that it is something that is a part of our family and that is our lot in life." Well, this fits the above scriptures perfectly. But there is good news! The Bible says that cursed is everything that hangs on a tree. Jesus Christ hung on a tree (known as a cross) for anyone who accepts him as Savior. Because of all his suffering and him coming down to earth as a man to take our sins, we can now walk and receive the blessing of HIS generation, that is, of the Father, Son, and Holy Spirit. God is a god of grace because he ends with saying that he shows love to a thousand generations to those in our family line that have obeyed him. Thank God that he has given us a way of escape through his love. Now think about the fact that God sent his only son Jesus to do away with the curse of sin. When Jesus gave up his life on the cross, he sacrificed himself through the shedding of his blood for all who would believe that he is the son of God and that his blood cleanses us. That is God showing his love to us through the generations because we as Christians have been adopted into the family of God and are of the seed of Abraham. Where are you today? If you are not walking in the blessing of God, then repent of your sin, receive Jesus in your heart, renounce Satan and accept that you are blessed. Praise the Lord!

Prayer: Father God, thank you for letting me be a part of a family that you are showing your love through. Thank you that Jesus is not only my savior, but he is my older brother and I receive the blessings of a thousand generations to those that love you. Thank you that the curse of sin and iniquity is broken and that I live under your love and blessings, in Jesus name, amen.

DAY 3

Nehemiah 9.17

They refused to listen and failed to remember the miracles you performed among them. They became stiff-necked and in their rebellion appointed a leader in order to return to their slavery. But you are a forgiving God, gracious and compassionate; slow to anger and abounding in love. Therefore you did not desert them...

I guess it is with human nature that we can so easily forget what God has done for us. It has happened to all of us. I remember several years ago things weren't going the way that I would have wanted in my ministry. It didn't look like I was moving toward the vision that God had shown me years before. So I decided to take things into my own hands. I don't know why we think we know more than God, the one who created us. But the flesh and the influence of the world make us think that. Of course, Satan plays the leading role. Praise the Lord because he ignores our stupidity and still shows us his unfailing love. Why don't you just repent of your self-focused ways and stubbornness and ask God to extend his grace to you again in this season in your life? Remember, I had to repent too. Thank you Jesus that you continue to be full of grace and mercy, amen! We can be so excited about God's blessing and hand in our lives at the moment, but then just weeks later we get into our complaining mode and try to take things into our own hands because of the sin nature within us. We fail to be full of gratitude. Yes, there were many miracles performed on Israel's behalf and they quickly wanted to once again become their own boss. But let's not be too hard on them. Let's look at our own lives. How many times have God asked us to trust him for even smaller things, but yet we only look to ourselves only to fail in the long run? Yet had we looked to God, who is the author and finisher of our faith, we would be daily walking in the victory that comes through trust and obedience in him. After all is said and done, we can still go to God and he will be there waiting with full compassion and forgiveness and slow to become angry with us. He is the God of grace.

Prayer: Father God, I come before you in the name of Jesus and by the blood of Jesus. The blood gives me the right to come before you boldly to receive mercy in my time of need. Lord, I repent of not listening to you and following my own ways. Forgive me! I know my ways are not your ways, but your ways are higher. Lord, because of Jesus I can have your higher ways- the way of righteousness and holiness. I receive it now and from this day onward I walk in blessings of obedience and humility before you, in Jesus name, amen!

DAY 4

Psalm 13.5

But I trust in your unfailing love; my heart rejoices in your salvation.

In this scripture the main words that jump off the page for me are trust, love, heart, and salvation, but when we look at it fully it takes on greater meaning. God is love and his love is unfailing and we should simply trust him and HIS love. When we understand that concept or principle, our heart will naturally rejoice. We know that God loved us so much that he sent his son, Jesus Christ, that we would receive salvation instead of damnation. Naturally trusting and rejoicing is ideal, but we are not able to trust, love and rejoice in God naturally without first building a relationship with him. It is a process that happens over time similar to a relationship between parents and children. Initially, the child seems to automatically know that the parent cares for him or her when things don't always go the way they want it to. But when things don't go their way; for example, when the child cries and mommy doesn't respond as quickly as she used to, or when the baby is hungry and is not fed right away. Initially, the baby might inwardly begin to wonder if it has been abandoned. I know that is kind of oversimplifying things, but I hope you understand my point, which is that over time with a good parent the child will begin to realize that even though the mother doesn't always come to its rescue when it thinks she should or when the child wants them to, mommy will be there right on time. It will not die and it will not starve. After a while as the child increases with age, the child learns that the parent loves them and will do what is best for them. I see the same with God as Father and us. Looking at my personal story, I always had a reverence and respect for God as creator, but had to learn to trust him as Father, friend, provider, etc. Now, I can truly say, through life's trials and tests and with age, I have come to rejoice in my salvation and to trust in God's unfailing love. Though many times, I have failed him; HE has never failed me. Trust him today and I promise, if you do, HE will do the same for you.

Prayer: Father God, forgive me of not trusting, loving and rejoicing in you as I should. Help me and show me your unfailing love as I live day to day. Let me rejoice in not only the big victories, but the small ones in the same manner. Thank you for saving me, in Jesus name, amen!

DAY 5

Psalm 136.1

Give thanks to the LORD, for he is good. "His love endures forever."

This is one of my favorite scriptures because it is one of thanksgiving and praise for the goodness of God. While doing missionary service in Asia, one of my sisters in the Lord said, "You are always thanking Jesus!" I was not surprised by her saying this. I make it a practice of thanking God throughout the day for all his blessings. But what startled me was that it had become such a part of my character and speech that it was really that noticeable to others. Are you thankful to God for all he has done in your life? What do people hear when they are around you? Why not let it be "His love endures forever"?

Prayer: Father God, thank you for all your blessings that you have poured upon me. I am thankful for life, health, strength, prosperity, peace and every good thing which comes from you my father. I know without a doubt that your love endures forever. Lord Jesus, let that forever be an answer to my prayers- your love endures forever, in Jesus name, amen!

DAY 6

Proverbs 3.3

Let love and faithfulness never leave you; bind them around your neck, write them on the tablet of your heart.

Down through the years when I had a key or something of similar size that was important to me as I was going about my duties in a particular day, I needed to have a place to keep it close to me so that it would not be lost and no one else would be able to get it. So in those cases when I wore clothing with no pockets or didn't want to take the chance of the item slipping out of my pocket I would put it on a secure chain around my neck. After doing this, I felt reassured that it was not only safe, but quickly accessible to me when I needed it. This is the message that the writer of Proverbs wants us to get concerning love and faithfulness. We should put it in a place so near to us that we would be constantly reassured and reminded that we are to love and be faithful continually. Then the author of Proverbs extends it further by saying that it should be written on the tablet of our heart. It is one thing to write it in the notebook tablet and when we are finished studying we can easily put that away on the shelf. It is quite different when it is written on the tablet of our heart. The word becomes a part of our inner being which gives us the ability to be full of love and faithfulness. But how can you really bind them around your neck and on the tablet of your heart? Well, this comes by daily meditating and purposely obeying the word of God. When you become full on the inside there will be an overflow on the outside that will affect not only you, but those around you also.

Prayer: Father, with your help and my willingness, I will allow love and faithfulness to be a part of my inner being so that I can experience your fullness and give it out to those around me. I want to thank you for showing me the importance of love and faithfulness in the Kingdom of God, in Jesus name, amen!

DAY 7

Proverbs 10.12

Hatred stirs up dissension, but love covers over all wrongs.

This reminds me of the love of a mother to her child. She will go to the very depths of hell for the one that she has carried in her womb for nine long months. Only one who has been there can truly understand this kind of love. I liken this to the nurturing love of God, the father, which goes even beyond a mother's love. Have you ever experienced God's love? There have been times in my life when I was not in my right mind and God, the Father, in his mothering nature was holding me near to his heart when I didn't even know it. When did I know it? I knew it when the enemy's stronghold was released from my mind and then I was able to know that when I was in my worst mental, physical, emotional, financial and spiritual state God was there and he covered up the multitude of my sins. And God is there holding you right now in all your joy and sadness, in all your blessings, and sin, in everything and in every place.

Prayer: Father, in the name of Jesus Christ, I pray for your dear one reading this right now. Show them your love. Show them that there is no god like you. Show them that you are the one, true God. Show them that there is nothing they can do that will make you leave them Lord, in Jesus name, amen!

DAY 8

Ecclesiastes 3.8

….a time to love and a time to hate, a time for war and a time for peace.

In the world there are times and seasons that come and go both in the natural, in politics, in education, in business and in every other arena. This even includes times of change in our individual lives and families. Even God himself has experienced love, hate, war and peace. The writer of this verse confirms this in our scripture verse for today. With God, all times are based upon the foundation of love. What do I mean? Everything that God does or allows is because of his love. But that is not always the case for us as humanity. We usually don't hate sin because it is sin, but we hate because we have allowed the wicked spirit of hatred to take over our lives. That is not founded on God's foundation of love. So today, I want you to examine your heart and ask the Holy Spirit to show you everything in your heart and life that is not rooted in love.

Prayer: Hello daddy, I want to come in your presence now. First, I want you to clean my heart of everything that is at enmity with you, of all sin. Lord, I repent of everything that you have shown me. (Take a few minutes of silent mediation so God can speak to your heart-then repent) Father, I thank you for forgiving me of my sinful heart. Put me on the foundation and in the season of love now, in Jesus name, amen!

DAY 9

Song of Solomon 2.4

He has taken me to the banquet hall, and his banner over me is love.

Wow! Isn't that so romantic for those romanticists out there? This is from the "Love" man himself, Solomon. So immediately we know that it probably has to do with love and/or wisdom. A banquet hall is a place where celebration takes place and I can imagine that the hall is packed with people all dressed in their best attire with a spirit of excitement because of the activity at hand. When a banner is placed over something it is for its protection. That brings me to what I want to say about love. Love protects. God protects. Are you going through a situation right now in your life where you feel like you have no covering from the trials of life? Well, Jesus is your covering. You are covered by the blood of Jesus. You are covered by the word of God. You are covered by the Holy Spirit. And all of the covering is built on the foundation of love.

Prayer: Heavenly Father, thank you so much for your banner of love covering me. Your word says that love covers a multitude of sin. Lord you don't cover my sin up so that others don't see it, BUT you wipe it away as if it has never happened. PRAISE THE LORD! Thank you LORD for your covering of love for me; Father, I love you because you first loved me, in Jesus name, amen!

DAY 10

Isaiah 38.17

Surely it was for my benefit that I suffered such anguish. In your love you kept me from the pit of destruction; you have put all my sins behind your back.

In life we have many challenges and setbacks which can often cause us to become angry not only at ourselves, but others and worst of all, sometimes we even become angry with God. Have you ever been there? Well, I will be honest and say I definitely have. And it was in God's grace that he allowed me to continue to have life in the midst of my arrogance to be angry with him the creator and sustainer of all things. As the writer of this verse has stated, "it was for my benefit." What is the benefit? It is simply maturity. Without the pressures of life, our own character won't be exposed and we won't push into knowing who God is. God is teaching you to have an intimate relationship with him. God is so good that even when we are foolish and have the audacity to become angry with him or rebel against a number of other things, he is not only still there, but still forgiving in the greatness of his love.

Prayer: Father, thank you that you never will stop loving me as I continue to mature and get to know you, in Jesus name, amen!

DAY 11

Isaiah 54.10

Though the mountains be shaken and the hills be removed, yet my unfailing love for you will not be shaken nor my covenant of peace be removed," says the LORD, who has compassion on you.

Today there is much opposition and confusion in the world. As I think about the years that I have been allowed upon this earth to have breath, each year becomes more chaotic and ungodly. Surely the Lord Jesus is coming quickly! But while I wait it gives me an assurance and confidence to know that I am not of this earthly-worldly system, but from the Kingdom of God, led by the King of Kings himself, Jesus Christ. Without faith in God and the Holy Spirit living within, it is easy to be comfortable living in the system of the world. But I thank God always that as believers in Christ Jesus we are only sojourners here in this land. It doesn't matter how difficult things are, or will become in the days to come, God will be there for us with his unfailing love. So we will not be shaken but relax in the peace of God.

Prayer: Lord God, as I sit here during this time of devotion today, I am experiencing so much of your peace because my anchor is in no one else but you Lord Jesus. You are my rock! You are my strong shield! You are my pavilion! You are my peace! You are my anchor! YOUARE you! Amen!

DAY 12

Isaiah 63.9

In all their distress he too was distressed, and the angel of his presence saved them. In his love and mercy he redeemed them; he lifted them up and carried them all the days of old.

Isn't that beautiful? Whatever we are going through in our lives, God is there. He is surrounding us making sure no detriment comes to us. Aren't we often just like the children of Israel in that somehow we know God is always with us, but we don't seem to get it until we have been in the fire and look back in retrospect over time? Then it hits us that though we turned our hearts from the Lord, he was still there. What a loving God! How many people do you know in your life that has ALWAYS been there for you? I mean someone who never even thought for a moment of leaving you. If we are honest, then we would have to say no one. I would imagine even for those who are deeply in love and have been married for many years somewhere back there you had a fleeting thought that maybe, just maybe, I will leave. BUT God is not like that. He is our redeemer, our lifter, and our carrier. SELAH!

Prayer: Father, today, I just want to thank you for being there when no one else was and for being here when no one else is. Amen!

DAY 13

Jeremiah 31.3

The LORD appeared to us in the past, saying: "I have loved you with an everlasting love; I have drawn you with loving-kindness.

To love with an everlasting love is astounding. This love implies that it lasts forever. As we study the lives of the children of Israel over the years and even the Jewish people today, we can see that the hand of God is with them. Though all Christians don't agree, I believe they have a special place in God's heart. It is kind of like being a mother with a wayward child. No matter what that child has done it can never be so awful that you totally lose your heart and not hurt for them and want them back in whatever condition they come. I believe that is not only how God is with Israel, but also with us since we have been made a part of the Kingdom of God through the blood of Jesus Christ. The Gentile Christians are now sons of God. Remember, everlasting is really "lasting ever." If God loves us with an everlasting love, do you think he might want to experience an everlasting love FROM us as well?

Prayer: Lord Jesus, thank you for loving me forever! Lord, no one on this earth can love me forever in the way that you do. You love me in the midst of all my weaknesses, confusion, doubt, and sin. So, I want to say thank you. Lord Jesus, teach me how to love the way you love me. Amen!

DAY 14

Lamentations 3.22

Because of the LORD's great love we are not consumed, for his compassions never fail.

God's faithfulness of love is so great! I am reminded of the classic hymn "Great is Thy Faithfulness." That is so true. We are where we are now because of God's great love. He is forever compassionate. And I hear someone saying, "Well, my situation is not so good. So you are saying that God put me in this situation?" Absolutely not! Often we are in the predicament that we are in because of bad choices, but it could also be because of satanic opposition and interference in our lives. But what I am saying is that if you have a sound mind and you still have breath then praise the Lord that it is not over yet. Remember, when we are at our worst, God shows us HIS best! He gives us great love and great compassion!

Prayer: Sweet Jesus, thank you for your unfailing love and compassion for me over the years. You have loved me when I didn't love myself. You showed me how to love me. Now Lord, show me how to love others the way you loved me. Amen!

DAY 15

Lamentations 3.31-32

For men are not cast off by the Lord forever. Though he brings grief, he will show compassion, so great is his unfailing love.

It is hard to think that God would cast us off. But the word says he does. BUT I really like the last word in verse 31-forever. If we look at it from a New Testament (Jesus) perspective we know that God does not cast us off, but the sin we allow in our lives brings that distance between God and us. We must live in the realm of getting rid of sin as soon as it comes, but even better, keep flowing in the grace of God by keeping that love affair of communication with him so that sin has to stop at your door. Darkness cannot enter the place where light lives. God is compassionate; therefore, I am compassionate because God lives inside of me through the Holy Spirit. When God hurts, I hurt. When God shows mercy, I show mercy. When God loves, I love. When God forgives, I forgive. When God grieves, I grieve. When God gives grace, I give grace. HIS love is surely unfailing. So, I too, should practice unfailing love.

Prayer: Lord Jesus, thank you for always showing compassion and grace to me even when I cast you off willingly by my rebellion and sin. Thank you for your love. Amen!

DAY 16

Joel 2.13

Rend your heart and not your garments. Return to the LORD your God, for he is gracious and compassionate, slow to anger and abounding in love, and he relents from sending calamity.

This reminds me of the scripture "But the LORD said to Samuel, "Do not consider his appearance or his height, for I have rejected him. The LORD does not look at the things man looks at. Man looks at the outward appearance, but the LORD looks at the heart." (1 Samuel 16.7, NIV) God wants US! He doesn't want our religious rituals. He doesn't want us to appease him to try to get what we want. Why do you think God wants our heart? Well, your heart is where the real "YOU" resides. Jesus said that what we speak out of our mouth is what is in our heart. The blessing for us is that God never gives up on us and God never fails us. He stands at the door of our heart knocking and waiting for us to repent, open our heart, and let him in.

Prayer: Lord Jesus, thanks for giving us a heart that has the ability to be full of your love. Help us to see what we DO daily to show ourselves, others, and even you how spiritual we are or how "not so bad" we are. Let us know it is not about doing, but about being a son of God. Thank you for your patience with us! Amen!

DAY 17

Micah 6.8

He has showed you, O man, what is good. And what does the LORD require of you? To act justly and to love mercy and to walk humbly with your God.

How beautiful this Scripture is! God has let us know what is good. And since God has shown us what is good, he is requiring us to act out and do and be that good that he has shown us. God wants us to live righteously, honestly, show mercy and practice the spirit of humility. In the not too distant past, the Lord reminded me, as I was transitioning into another level of ministry that the key to me rising up in him is to be OBEDIENT and HUMBLE. This was a life-transforming statement for me. I knew I should be obedient and humble; however, if God had to remind me of those two things it meant that at the current time either I wasn't obedient and humble or I had received that lesson after many years of life trials and now I could receive those words from him. Well, to me, the latter reason resonated within my soul. I immediately received God's word and saw even more favor come into my life. I encourage you be righteous, merciful, and humble and you will receive more of God's grace and favor in your life.

Prayer: Father God, thank you for your loving kindness and tender mercies. You have been so good to me when I wasn't even good to myself. Lord, I surrender all, in Jesus name, amen!

DAY 18

Zechariah 8.19

This is what the LORD Almighty says: "The fasts of the fourth, fifth, seventh and tenth months will become joyful and glad occasions and happy festivals for Judah. Therefore love truth and peace."

Fasting was and is a religious ritual in many religions and is done for many reasons. Specifically, as we trace the history of fasting in the Bible and the Hebrew people (Israelites-Jews) they fasted as a sign of distress, grief, repentance, and ultimately hoping God would have mercy upon them and help their situations. In the Law of Moses the fast was only required on The Day of Atonement in which they later called the Day of Fasting or The Fast. This was a national feast that the Israelites sought the Lord to forgive them for their sins. Fasting was a religious, traditional ritual for Israel, but God gave a word through the Prophet Zechariah, whose primary message was that Jesus, the Messiah was coming in all his glory. Zechariah's message in this verse is that God is going to turn your sad fasts into times of joyful, glad and happy occasions. Not to oversimplify this scripture and its context, but to glean a nugget from this; God is saying that I have heard your prayers and seen your good deeds and you will receive my peace knowing that you are loved by me. Have you ever been in a situation where you have seemingly given all to the Lord, but it seemed as if when you call out to him there is no answer? Well, you are in great company because that happens to everyone. God often uses everything in our lives to purify our motives and to create in us a humble and dependent heart upon him. But I want to encourage you today that your day of gladness is near. God will turn your mourning into laughter and give you increased strength through the joy of the Lord.

Prayer: Father God, thank you for turning my sadness into joy. I know that my day of deliverance is near. Lord Jesus, I will praise you each day and continue to love as you continue to turn my heart toward you. I love your truth and your peace, in Jesus name, amen.

DAY 19

Matthew 5.44

But I tell you: Love your enemies and pray for those who persecute you.

Well, as I have read in the Bible, this is a hard saying, meaning easier said than done. How many of you will agree? It is true that one cannot do this in his or her own strength. It takes the supernatural power of God to love your enemies. It actually seems a little bit far out to pray and love someone who has a gun at your head, a knife at your throat or who is writing or speaking something totally against who you really are. When a believer gets to the point where they can pray and love those who are trying to literally destroy them in every way, shape and form, then you had better believe they are from another world. They have been transformed by the blood of Jesus Christ. But as we continue through the upcoming days and years, God will be requiring more love and forgiveness for those who are in the darkness that have not yet seen the light. This is the way of Christ and our model example. Can you do it? No, not in your strength; but YES you can in HIS strength.

Prayer: Father God, thank you for the privilege and honor to represent you in this earthly world through unconditional love and infinite forgiveness through the work of the Holy Spirit within me, in Jesus name, amen!

DAY 20

Luke 16.13

"No servant can serve two masters. Either he will hate the one and love the other, or he will be devoted to the one and despise the other. You cannot serve both God and Money."

As I am reading this scripture now I think about those who have many husbands or wives (including those who have several boyfriends or girlfriends). How is it possible that you can have a divided heart? Actually, I believe when one tries to divide his or her heart then actually there is no love going anywhere. When we try to give our heart to Christ (the kingdom of God) and then give it to Satan (the god of this world) we are trying to serve two masters. God lets us know that our heart cannot be divided. When we try to love both then we end up loving neither. You either love good or evil. You either love God's word or the words of the world. You either love righteousness or evil. You either love God or Satan. Your actions show where your love is, not necessarily your speech.

Prayer: Father God, teach me how to love only you. I only want you to be my master. Though sometimes I find myself tangled up in the snares of this world, my heart really is not at peace with that and I know that you are calling me to be free of the entanglement of the world's system and to come forth totally to you Father in the kingdom of God. Help me to come toward you as I determine in my heart to do what is right in your eyes, not my own, in Jesus name, amen!

DAY 21

John 15.17

This is my command: Love each other.

Whose command is this? This is the command of Jesus. He did not say that I hope you all love each other, or it would be really nice if you all would learn to love one another. NO, NO, NO. Jesus said that he COMMANDS us to love one another. When someone in authority gives a command then it is something that MUST be done and if it is not heeded to then there will be unpleasant consequences. If we think about it in our modern day, then we can see the visual of a military commander giving orders to those under him in his unit or in other words those under his command. Speaking of command, I think about the centurion in the New Testament who had a servant that he really respected that was about to die. This is what the centurion told his servants to say to Jesus, "For I myself am a man under authority, with soldiers under me. I tell this one, 'Go,' and he goes: and that one, 'Come,' and he comes. I say to my servant, 'Do this,' and he does it." (Luke 7:1-10) Two things I notice here. First, the centurion's servant quickly obeyed their master and secondly, the centurion knew how authority worked and he knew Jesus walked in that authority of command as well. As Kingdom citizens, we also know Jesus is one of authority and we have to obey his commands.

Prayer: Lord, thank you for your command for me to love as you have loved. I not only love you, but I love others too, especially my Christian family, in Jesus name, amen!

DAY 22

Romans 8.35

Who shall separate us from the love of Christ? Shall trouble or hardship or persecution or famine or nakedness or danger or sword?

Have you been tried in your faith? If your answer is no then my question to you is have you been tried in your life? We all will face all kinds of life hardships, but as a believer the question is will we let any of the challenges of life challenge our faith? There should never be a "who" or "what" that causes us to lose our faith. Well, I must admit that I have come pretty close to losing all hope. The different trials and tests that we go through can suck the life right out of us. One of the lowest times of my life when I thought I could not go on another day, I had actually given up on religion and was trying to give up on God's call on my life. BUT that is when God stepped in and used the little bit of hope that I had left and cultivated that seed and with my participation caused it to germinate and hope budded and over time my life was in full bloom again. Notice I said over time. One thing that I am grateful for is that God did not allow me to give up on HIM. Nothing was able to separate me from his love.

Prayer: O' Father, how I love you because you loved me in the midst of all my troubles and hardships. You kept your promise and did not forsake me. Lord, I promise I will never let anything separate me from your love, in Jesus name, amen!

DAY 23

1 Corinthians 2.9

However, as it is written: "No eye has seen, no ear has heard, no mind has conceived what God has prepared for those who love him."

Do you love him? Really, do you love him? If you love him God has many precious promises for you both now in this world and in the world to come. It is beyond what we can imagine with our finite human ability. God is too big and too incomprehensible for us to even begin to think that we can describe HIM or know his ways beyond what he himself shows us. We marvel in our ability to use our sense of seeing, hearing and thinking. It amazes me to notice how even the most intellectual of human beings will try to think that they know God's every move. Interesting huh? One thing I am sure of and that is God's word is truth and God does not lie. So he has something very special prepared for us both now and in the future. Do you want it? Then follow the requirement-LOVE HIM!

Prayer: Lord Jesus, I love you. Teach me how to love you even more. Lord, I want to receive everything that you have prepared for me both now and always. Thank you in advance for all your precious and valuable gifts to me, in Jesus name, amen!

DAY 24

2 Corinthians 2.4

For I wrote you out of great distress and anguish of heart and with many tears, not to grieve you but to let you know the depth of my love for you.

Apostle Paul is writing to his beloved Corinthians church. This is his second letter to the Corinthians whom he loves. In the first letter he wrote very strongly because there were issues that he had to confront that were not fitting for those called as followers of Christ. He had to lay a foundation of holy expectations and guides for the church. It seems that Paul wanted them to know that all that he had said and done is because of his love for them. Have you ever been there? Where? Have you ever had to deliver some tough or hard to swallow news to someone that you loved? Not easy, is it? But it is often very much needed. The Bible says that even God chastens those whom he loves. Think about it. Do you really spend all your valuable time or money on something or someone that you don't love? Well, that is exactly the point that Paul is making in his writing. What is valuable to us, we love. We are valuable to God. Question: Is God valuable to you?

Prayer: Father, thank you for your discipline for me because you love me. Although sometimes your training is painful, I know you do it because it is good for me so that I may mature because you love me so much, in Jesus name, amen!

DAY 25

Galatians 5.6

For in Christ Jesus neither circumcision nor uncircumcision has any value. The only thing that counts is faith expressing itself through love.

This is a beautiful Scripture. It cuts right through religion. Excuse the pun. (cut through as relating to cutting in circumcision) The writer of Galatians is saying that Christ places value in our faith that is expressed through love. This is saying a lot here. First, everyone who comes to Christ must have faith. Secondly, love only comes through faith. Faith and love are partners. If someone says they have great faith, but they don't show it through love, then we would be correct to doubt their faith. Even so, if someone says they have so much love, but they don't show it by actions (faith), then we are right to question their love. Though circumcision is still practiced today and mainly for reasons of hygiene, it is not needed to become a follower of Christ. At the time the Jews who practiced circumcision because of Jewish law also wanted to impose it upon the Gentile believers. But Paul is saying that is not necessary, but only "faith expressing itself through love." The blood and flesh of Jesus has replaced the blood and flesh of man. We are freed from empty rituals. When Jesus sets us free through his love we are totally free.

Prayer: Lord God, thank you for freeing humanity from lifeless rituals of circumcision. Thank you for circumcising my heart and cutting away all impurities from my inward person. I will let my faith express itself through love for you and others, in Jesus name, amen!

DAY 26

Ephesians 4.15

Instead, speaking the truth in love, we will in all things grow up into him who is the Head, that is, Christ.

How can we grow up in Christ? We must speak the truth in love. What is truth? The Word of God is truth. So we must speak the truth of the Word. There are many in the world today speaking what they claim is truth, though I doubt they are claiming that they are speaking it in love. Many today don't believe in the absolute truth of the Bible but elevate the logical mind and its insights foremost over God's word. But as it relates to the body of Christ, God has commanded us that we need to tell our sisters and brothers the truth of the word as it relates to their situation. For example, if someone has been diagnosed with cancer, do we just feel sorry for them and let them dwindle away as one with no hope? No, we speak the truth of God's word in love to them and tell them that Jesus took our sickness and disease on the cross of Calvary and because of that we can be healed physically in our bodies just like we are spiritually in our souls. Beloved, I admonish you that you begin to speak and teach and believe only what God says in his word which is absolute truth and you can bank on it.

Prayer: Jesus, thank you for giving me the truth of your word. I walk in it right now, in Jesus name, amen!

DAY 27

Philippians 1.9-11

And this is my prayer: that your love may abound more and more in knowledge and depth of insight, so that you may be able to discern what is best and may be pure and blameless until the day of Christ, filled with the fruit of righteousness that comes through Jesus Christ—to the glory and praise of God.

And I second that prayer. Beloved it is God's desire that you know HIM. It is one of the deepest desires of the Lord's heart. He knows you and loves you, but something is missing in that relationship between the two of you when you are not growing in your love and desire for him. God's love is the deepest love that you can ever experience. He is preparing you for his arrival when he will meet you face to face in all of HIS glory. Wow! How awesome is that? Sweet. And that is exactly how he wants the fruit of your life to be. He wants it to be sweet and full of righteousness and for you to desire to know HIM even more. Do you want to know him more? I believe you. Let us pray.

Prayer: Dear Jesus, let my love grow deeper and deeper in you. Holy Spirit, teach me the deepness of God's love for me and the world. Even today, let me experience the depth of your love, in Jesus name, amen!

DAY 28

Colossians 1.5

We always thank God, the Father of our Lord Jesus Christ, when we pray for you, because we have heard of your faith in Christ Jesus and of the love you have for all the saints--the faith and love that spring from the hope that is stored up for you in heaven and that you have already heard about in the word of truth, the gospel.

One of the trademarks of Paul and one in which I really admire is that his teachings always are surrounded by faith, hope and love. If you think about it that is what the Christian faith is all about-Faith, Hope and Love. But from the Scriptures we know that faith works by love. In other words they are tightly connected. Our hope is based upon the premises that this earth is temporary and everything that is in it, so we have a heavenly hope of going to an eternal place of everlasting peace, provision, and love. That is our hope. Beloved, when all else fails-don't give up hope. We must encourage each other as sisters and brothers in Christ as we hope and wait through faith and in love the second coming of our Lord and Savior, Jesus Christ.

Prayer: Jesus my hope is in you! Thank you Lord! Amen!

DAY 29

1 Thessalonians 3.12

May the Lord make your love increase and overflow for each other and for everyone else, just as ours does for you.

What is love? The best definition of the God kind of love, which I believe is the only true definition is found in 1 Corinthian 13.3-8. "And though I bestow all my goods to feed the poor, and though I give my body to be burned, but have not love, it profits me nothing. Love suffers long and is kind; love does not envy; love does not parade itself, is not puffed up; does not behave rudely, does not seek its own, is not provoked, thinks no evil; does not rejoice in iniquity, but rejoices in the truth; bears all things, believes all things, hopes all things, endures all things. Love never fails. But whether there are prophecies, they will fail; whether there are tongues, they will cease; whether there is knowledge, it will vanish away." The most importance thing to remember about love is it is focused outwardly. Now, this is totally contrary to how "the world" would define love. According to the movies of Hollywood love is almost always about the one who wants it and who almost would do anything to get it. That is not real love. That seems more like dysfunctionalism and insecurity. But how do we make true love increase so that it does overflow so naturally to others? Simply, make sure we keep our love tank full of God's love by reading the word, staying filled with the Spirit, spending personal time in prayer and fellowship with Jesus and other believers.

Prayer: Lord Jesus, thank you for filling my love tank daily as I continue to receive your unconditional love. I know that I can do many things for your kingdom but without love all of it is without your grace. Fill me again and again Lord, in Jesus name, amen!

DAY 30

2 Thessalonians 3.5

May the Lord direct your hearts into God's love and Christ's perseverance.

One of the Bible versions that I like reading during my devotion time is the New Living Translation. It speaks more deeply to my soul. 2 Thessalonians 3.5 in this translation says, "May the Lord bring you into an ever deeper understanding of the love of God and the endurance that comes from Christ." Beloved, that is my prayer for you. My greatest desire for people is that they would know Jesus through a personal relationship with the Holy Spirit. I desire that you know him intimately as your friend and God as your father. God desires that too. The writer of Thessalonians shares this desire with us in the scripture verse here. When life begins to wear on you, then you can be comforted in the fact that Christ is there with you all the way. As you travel the road of life with him you will also grow in your love for him and he will shine his love through you to others.

Prayer: Lord, direct my heart deeper and deeper in your love and help me to continue daily in pursuing your love and sonship, in Jesus name, amen!

DAY 31

Revelation 2.4

Yet I hold this against you: You have forsaken your first love.

This would be devastating to hear God say this to you, right? I agree and it was. You see, before I really knew this scripture existed God spoke that word to me when I was putting any and everything in my life above him. He actually said that he would remove his candlestick and he let me know he meant "Holy Spirit." So basically, God was saying that he would take his presence away from me if I did not repent and make him number one in my life. How long do you think it took me to set my house in order and put God first again? You guessed well. Not long at all. Since then I have never forgotten that word and it guides me daily to keep Jesus as my first love. Did I miss it again after that? You bet, but with quick repentance. Is that a new concept to you, having Jesus as your "first love"? Well, he wants to be that to you too. It simply means to put him above all else and above all others and he will direct your ways so that everything and everyone else in your life will be in the right place. Receive Jesus as your first love or return to him as your first love.

Prayer: Jesus, always keep me as your first love. Keep me in step with you and the Holy Spirit. We are a symphony and you are the leader, in Jesus name!

PRAYER OF SALVATION

If you are not a born-again Christian

Dear Lord Jesus, come into my heart right now. Lord, I confess that I have sinned. But you say if I admit that I have sinned, have a change of heart and actions, you will forgive my sins and make me clean, make me whole. I believe that. Thank you, Lord Jesus for cleansing and saving me. I am now a born-again Christian. Amen!

PRAYER OF REDEDICATION

If you are a believer, but are out of fellowship with the Lord

Dear Lord Jesus, forgive me for turning my back on you and for not been faithful. I confess that I have sinned. But you say that if I confess my sins, you would forgive me. I believe that. I turn away from my sinful actions. Thank you Lord Jesus for forgiving me, making me whole and giving me another chance. I am now restored back in fellowship with you. Amen!

PRAYER FOR BAPTISM WITH THE HOLY SPIRIT

You need more power and strength

Dear Lord Jesus, I am a Christian. Thank you for saving me. Lord, I want to experience the baptism with the Holy Spirit. The Holy Spirit came into my heart when I became a Christian, but I want to experience more power. I repent of all sins and come before you with a pure heart. You say in your word that every good and perfect gift comes from above and that you give it freely. So baptize me now with the free gift of the Holy Spirit. I receive it now. I will open my mouth and let the tongues flow out by faith. In Jesus name, amen!

Other Books by *d Yvonne Shotwell*

How to Quickly Grow and Identify Godly Fruit: The Spiritual Path to Christian Maturity and Marriage

How to Quickly Grow and Identify Godly Fruit: The Workbook

A Guide to the Christian Life

Websites:

www.onlinenewyouniversity.com

www.prophetickingdomsolutions.com

www.hmvea.org